America's Game
New York Yankees

Paul Joseph

ABDO & Daughters
PUBLISHING

Published by Abdo & Daughters, 4940 Viking Dr., Suite 622, Edina, MN 55435.

Cover photo: Allsport
Interior photos: Wide World Photo, pages 1, 7, 11, 12, 15, 16, 21, 23, 24, 25, 28.
Allsport, page 5.

Edited by Kal Gronvall

Library of Congress Cataloging–in–Publication Data

Joseph, Paul, 1970-
  New York Yankees / Paul Joseph
      p. cm. — (America's game)
  Includes index.
  Summary: Focuses on key players and events in the history of the New York Yankees, who have won the World Series nearly every five years of their ninety-three-year Major League Baseball history.
  ISBN 1-56239-673-0
  1. New York Yankees (Baseball team)—History—Juvenile literature. [1. New York Yankees (Baseball team) 2. Baseball—History.] I. Title. II. Series.
GV875.N4J67 1997
796.357' 64' 097471—dc20   96-23089
                                                          CIP
                                                           AC

Contents

New York Yankees

No other franchise in Major League Baseball history has been as successful as the New York Yankees. In their 93-year existence, the Yankees have been in the World Series an average of every three years and have won the World Series nearly every five years.

The New York Yankees franchise began in 1903. They started off slowly, not winning their first American League Championship until 1921. But after that title, they dominated professional baseball. From 1921 to 1981, the Yankees won the American League (AL) title 33 times, and were World Champions 22 times.

And then in 1996, the Yankees captured their 23rd World Series title. The Yankees became the sentimental favorite behind their skipper, Joe Torre. In a year that had many ups and downs, the Yanks played with heart, determination, and guts in bringing another championship to New York.

The Yankees were a true dynasty, but they actually had four separate dynasties. But this great franchise struggled in the beginning. They played in the second-class American League, and were not even known as the Yankees at that time.

Facing page: Yankees' slugger Paul O'Neill gets a hit in a game against the Oakland Athletics.

The Highlanders

In 1903, two investors put up $18,000 to start the New York Highlanders. On April 20, 1903, more than 16,000 people showed up to witness the first-ever home game—and home victory—for the AL team called the Highlanders.

From 1903 to 1912, the Highlanders had good seasons—finishing second—and horrible seasons—finishing dead last. But most of the years they finished in the middle of the pack.

In 1913, the Highlanders officially changed their name to the Yankees—a nickname that newspaper reporters had called them for years. They also began playing in a new stadium—the Polo Grounds, home of the National League's New York Giants. Neither the name or stadium change helped them, as the Yankees finished in seventh place.

After another seventh-place finish in 1914, the team was sold for $460,000. With new ownership, the Yankees began to move up the ladder. In 1919, they finished third, only 7.5 games out of first place.

Then on January 5, 1920, the Yankees purchased the greatest player in baseball history.

The Babe

George Herman "Babe" Ruth was purchased from Boston for $125,000—more than double the amount ever given to any other baseball player to date.

The Babe inspired the Yankees to win many AL titles and World Series championships. Baseball fans nationwide jammed stadiums to watch Ruth hit home runs.

In 1920—his first season as a Yankee—the Babe batted .376 and led the league in RBIs (137), runs scored (158), walks (148), HRs (54), and a slugging percentage of .847—to this day the highest in the history of baseball!

Behind the awesome numbers of Babe Ruth, the Yankees finished the 1920 season in third place. But that was only the start for the Babe and the Yankees.

Babe Ruth watches one of his many home runs sail out of the ballpark.

In 1921, the Yankees won their first AL Championship behind Ruth's 59 home runs and 171 RBIs. In their first World Series, the Yankees were beaten by their crosstown rival, the New York Giants.

The Yankees had another great season in 1922. Led by Ruth, the Yankees grabbed another AL pennant and headed to their second-straight World Series. Again they were matched against the Giants, with the same unfortunate results.

But 1923 would be different. The Yankees would begin playing in a new stadium and take their first of many World Series Championships.

On opening day in 1923, the Yankees had a new place to play ball. Yankee Stadium was located in the Bronx, less than a mile from their old stadium. Babe Ruth was such an awesome player that he single-handedly turned the franchise around. As a result, Yankee Stadium became known as "The House That Ruth Built." The Babe, fittingly, smashed the first home run in the new stadium.

Ruth led the Yanks to a 4-1 opening-day victory. They went on to win the AL pennant for the third year in a row.

After losing the previous two World Series to their crosstown rival, the Giants, the Yankees won four games to two to capture their first World Series.

Yankee fans were hoping for another World Series title the next year, but they would be disappointed. In 1924 the Yankees just missed out, finishing in second place. And in 1925, the Yankees fell to seventh place, as Babe Ruth missed most of the season because of surgery.

In 1926, with the return of Ruth, the Yankees won the AL pennant. They didn't win the World Series that year, but the following year they put together an awesome lineup, and grabbed another World Series Championship.

The Greatest Team Ever

Many believe that the 1927 Yankees were the greatest baseball team of all time. Also known as the Bronx Bombers because of the team's hitting ability, the Yankees had a .489 slugging average and scored 975 runs—records that stand to this day.

The Yankees' team batting average was a whopping .307, and they led the league in every category except doubles (they were second) and stolen bases (they didn't need to).

Five out of their first six batters in the lineup hit over .300. Babe was second with a .356 average, and he broke his own major-league record in 1927 by smashing 60 home runs.

The leading hitter on the Yankees was the great Lou Gehrig. Gehrig ended the year with a .373 average, 175 RBIs, and 47 home runs.

The Bombers finished with 110 wins, played .714 ball, and outdistanced their closest competitor by 19 games. In the World Series, they swept the Pittsburgh Pirates in four games.

The Yankees had nearly the same awesome lineup in 1928, and with nearly the same results. They did struggle a little for the AL crown, but still won it. In the World Series, they swept the St. Louis Cardinals.

The Babe Goes Out With A Bang

In the following years the Yankees began to slide. Many believed that the team didn't care, or that they weren't disciplined enough. In 1931, the Yankees hired a new manager, Joe McCarthy. McCarthy coached the Yankees in a very businesslike fashion.

McCarthy's new approach worked well. The Yankees bounced back to second place in 1931, and grabbed another AL pennant in 1932, winning 107 games.

The 1932 World Series against the Chicago Cubs was Babe Ruth's last. In New York, the Yankees captured the first two games, and then the Series moved to Chicago.

In the third game, the 37-year old Ruth came up to the plate with two on in the first, and put the Yankees ahead 3-0 with a home run. In the fourth inning, he blasted his second home run. The Yanks went on to sweep the Cubs thanks to the Babe.

The Yankees, with the Babe, never got back to the World Series. But it didn't matter. Ruth had made his mark on Major League Baseball, and he will never be forgotten. Ruth retired in 1935. In 1936, the Babe was one of the first players inducted into the Baseball Hall of Fame.

The New Yankee Dynasty

Though the 1927 Yankee team was the greatest ever, the 1936 team was a close second. Beginning in 1936, the Yankees dominated the American League for the next six seasons.

Playing first base was Lou Gehrig. He had one of his "typical" great seasons, batting .354, smashing a league-leading 49 home runs, and driving in 152 runs. Then there was Bill Dickey, who also put up great numbers, hitting .362, with 107 RBIs. In fact, the Yanks as a team batted over .300.

Ace pitchers Red Ruffing (20 wins) and Monte Pearson (19 wins) led the Yanks on the hill. Together with solid pitching and awesome hitting, the team easily won the AL pennant by 19.5 games.

The biggest addition to the team in 1936 was a rookie from San Francisco, 21-year-old Joe DiMaggio. DiMaggio put in one of the best rookie seasons any baseball player has ever had. He batted .323, with 44 doubles, 15 triples, 29 home runs, and 125 RBIs. But this was only the start. DiMaggio continued that torrid pace throughout his career, bringing the Yankees championship after championship.

Right: Yankee outfielder Joe DiMaggio.

After beating the Giants four games to two in the 1936 World Series, many fans believed that this team could win two in row. But the Yanks proved that they were much better than that—they won four in a row!

In the 1937 World Series, the Yankees trounced the Giants again, winning four games to one. In 1938, they swept the Cubs. They did the same thing the following year to the Cincinnati Reds.

In 1940, the Yankees fell to third place, but they bounced back the next year, winning another World Series. But other events were much more in the forefront now. One was World War II. Many great baseball players had to fight in that war. And at home, death would claim one of the greatest players to wear a Yankee uniform.

Lou Gehrig batting during a 1937 game against the Boston Bees.

The Iron Horse Says Good-Bye

Lou Gehrig was known as the Iron Horse. He played in 2,130 consecutive games—a record that stood for nearly 56 years, until Cal Ripken, Jr., broke it in 1995.

It all ended for Gehrig on April 30, 1939, in Detroit. Clearly ailing, his weight falling, his uniform ill-fitting, his batting average .143, Gehrig told his manager to take him out of the lineup. The streak of 2,130 was over. No one suspected that Gehrig would never play again. He was struck down by "Lou Gehrig's disease," a serious illness that attacks the spine and causes paralysis.

Gehrig finished his career with a .340 batting average, a .632 slugging average, and 1,990 RBIs. His career slugging average and RBIs still rank third on the all-time list.

On July 4, 1939, the fans, players and coaches, both past and present, honored him with Lou Gehrig Appreciation Day, which to this day remains one of the most emotional events in sports history.

During the ceremony, Gehrig said to his baseball fans and friends, "What young man wouldn't give anything to mingle with such men for a single day as I have for all these years?... Today I consider myself the luckiest man on the face of the earth."

Gehrig's suffering ended with his death on June 2, 1941. He was only 37 years old.

Joe DiMaggio And His Streak

Although the Yankees won another World Series in 1941, it was "the streak" that everyone talked about. Joe DiMaggio had one of the most impressive achievements in baseball history—a 56-game hitting streak. Unlike other baseballs feats, a hitting streak must be accomplished on a day-by-day basis, with no breaks.

On May 15, 1941, DiMaggio began his streak with an unimpressive 1-for-4 afternoon against Chicago. When Joe hit in his 30th consecutive game, he became the first Yankee to reach that mark.

When the streak reached 40 on June 28 against Philadelphia, DiMaggio equaled the best Ty Cobb had ever done. In the July 1st doubleheader, Joe went 2-for-4 in the first game to set a new league record, and 1-for-3 in the nightcap. With a homer the next afternoon, DiMaggio reached 45 and broke the record. From then on the record was just Joe's to extend. And on he went. The Yankees went to Cleveland and DiMaggio went 3-for-4 with a double to run the hitting streak to 56. The next game he narrowly missed getting a hit.

For DiMaggio, 56 would forever be the magic number. And if that weren't enough, he went out the next day and began a 17-game hitting streak which, when it ended, gave him 73 out of 74!

In 1942, DiMaggio led the Yankees to another World Series, where they lost to the Cardinals four games to one. By 1943, most of baseball's stars had gone off to the war, including DiMaggio. The Yankees did, however, win the World Series with replacement players.

By 1946, the war was over and baseball was back in full swing. DiMaggio led the Yanks to the World Series in 1947. The Bronx Bombers won the hard-fought Series, four games to three over the Brooklyn Dodgers.

Joe DiMaggio, in his first official appearance with the Yankees, hits a single in a 1938 game against the Washington Senators.

Casey Stengel (left) and Mickey Mantle.

The 1950s

If the 1927 Yankees were the greatest team, and the 1936 team a close second, where do the 1950s' Yankees stand? They were led by manager Charles Dillon Stengel, also known as Casey.

Casey Stengel began his mission with the Yankees in 1949. He inherited a great team in need of leadership. Under Stengel, the Yankees fought hard and won the 1949 AL pennant. They easily won the World Series, four games to one over the Dodgers. But Stengel wasn't satisfied with just one World Championship.

In the next four years, Stengel led his team to World Series victories, giving New York five titles in a row—breaking the old record also held by the Yankees. The Yanks won the AL pennant in all but 2 of the 12 years under Stengel. They finished second in 1954 (with *only* 103 wins), and third in 1959. In all, the Bombers won seven World Championships!

After the second World Series victory under Stengel, Joe DiMaggio retired after one of the best careers in baseball history. The Yankees didn't miss a beat, though. One important reason for their continued success was 19-year-old slugging outfielder Mickey Mantle.

Mickey Mantle

The 1950s' Yankees will be remembered as one of the greatest baseball dynasties of all time. And of course, Casey Stengel will be remembered for his brilliant coaching. A hard-hitting catcher named Yogi Berra also helped the cause, winning three Most Valuable Player (MVP) Awards. And solid Yankee pitching kept opposing teams from scoring. This was highlighted by Don Larsen, who threw a perfect game in the 1956 World Series.

But in 1951, rookie outfielder Mickey Mantle joined the team. Not only was Mickey the key to the 1950s' dynasty, he also helped the Bombers in the 1960s. His glorious 18-year career included 12 AL pennants and 7 World Series titles.

"The Mick" could do it all. He could hit for average, always contending for the batting crown. (In 1956, he led the league with a .353 batting average.) He could steal bases, and was a solid outfielder.

But Mantle was known for his power. Four times he led the league in home runs, finishing his career with 536—eighth on the all-time list. He led the league six times in runs scored, and in RBIs once. For all of his accomplishments, Mickey Mantle was awarded the league's MVP three times, and was inducted into the Hall of Fame in 1974.

But Mickey didn't have to do all the home run hitting himself. In a trade in 1960, a young man joined the Yankees who would eventually break Babe Ruth's single-season home run record.

New York

In 1920, Babe Ruth had a slugging percentage of .847, the highest in baseball history.

In 1941 Joe DiMaggio had a hitting streak of 56 games in a row.

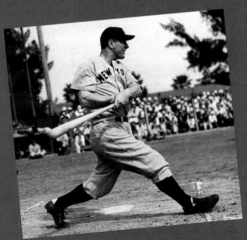

Lou Gehrig played in 2,130 consecutive games, a record that held until Cal Ripken, Jr., broke it in 1995.

Outfielder Mickey Mantle (right) finished his 18-year career with 536 home runs, eighth on the all-time list.

Yankees

In 1961, Roger Maris hit 61 home runs, breaking Babe Ruth's single-season record.

In the 1977 World Series, Reggie Jackson pounded out nine hits, five of which were home runs.

In each of his six seasons with the Yankees, Dave Winfield drove in more than 100 runs.

On September 4, 1993, Jim Abbott threw a no-hitter.

Maris Topples The Babe

After the incredible 1950s, the Yankees continued their winning ways in the early 1960s. Newcomer Roger Maris and Mickey Mantle led the way, and soon became known as the M&M boys.

Beginning in 1960, the M&M boys helped the Yankees win five-straight AL pennant crowns, and in 1961 and 1962, World Series Championships. But the real news in the early 1960s was the race to better Babe Ruth's home run record of 60. The two Yankees fighting it out were none other than the M&M boys.

In 1960, Maris belted 39 home runs and won the league's MVP. In 1961, Maris didn't get his first home run until the 11th game of the season. But then he caught fire, as did Mantle. The two were smashing them out of the ball park daily.

Mantle reached 54, and then was injured, forcing him to sit out until the playoffs. Maris continued on, tying Babe Ruth with his 60th home run in game 159. It came down to the final game and Maris still needed one home run to break the record. A fastball down the middle sent Maris' bat into motion. For a moment he stood in silence and watched the arc of the ball. Then he knew that baseball history had been made. Maris became the first man in history to hit 61 home runs in a single season. The Yankees won the game 1-0. It was also the team's 240th homer of the year, an all-time record.

After the Yankees won the pennant in 1964, the team began to break up. Some players retired. Others were traded. It was time to rebuild. The rebuilding would take time—and a lot of money.

Roger Maris hits his 61st homer of 1961, breaking Babe Ruth's single-season record.

 21

Mr. October

In 1973, a struggling Yankee franchise was sold to millionaire George Steinbrenner. With a lot of money in his pocket and good front-office people, Steinbrenner and his Yankees would go on to dominate the league in the late 1970s.

Some of the solid players already on the Yankees were Mel Stottlemyre, Thurman Munson, Roy White, Graig Nettles, and pitchers Sparky Lyle and Jim "Catfish" Hunter. The Yankees also made some great trades, acquiring first baseman Chris Chambliss, relief pitcher Dick Tidrow, and outfielder Mickey Rivers.

By 1976, the Yankees were back in the World Series. After being swept by the Cincinnati Reds, Steinbrenner knew that there was one important piece missing in the Yankee puzzle.

George Steinbrenner's biggest purchase in 1977 was high-priced and hard-hitting Reggie Jackson. Reggie had proven his worth with the Oakland Athletics, leading them to title after title.

In 1977, Jackson helped the Yankees win the AL pennant. He nearly single-handedly defeated the Dodgers in the World Series, four games to two. Reggie pounded out nine hits, five of which were home runs. (Three of those homers were in a row in the final game!) This is when Jackson became known as "Mr. October."

The Yankees repeated as World Champions in 1978, again defeating the Dodgers four games to two. New York was led that season by the awesome pitching of Ron Guidry, who had a 25-3 record and a 1.74 ERA, and by two great relievers, Goose Gossage and Sparky Lyle. In the Series, "Mr. October" kept up his numbers, smacking nine hits, driving in eight runs, and crushing two homers.

The Yankees made it back to the World Series in 1981, only to lose to the Dodgers. The Yankees continued to make deals and field good teams throughout the 1980s. They won more games than any other baseball franchise in the 1980s, but each year missed the mark, finishing often in second or third place.

Reggie Jackson watches a foul ball as he completes his swing in a game against the Boston Red Sox.

Dave Winfield hits a homer in a game against the Kansas City Royals.

Great Stars And Disappointment

The Yankees continued to attract big-name stars to their team, only to see disappointing finishes. A lot of it had to do with Steinbrenner, who was constantly fighting with his players—and changing managers more often than he changed his socks.

Dave Winfield was a real star for the Yankees, and proved it by driving in more than 100 runs in each of his six seasons. Don Mattingly put up stats matching those of the great Lou Gehrig.

The Yankees also added two great pitchers, Dave Righetti, who both started and relieved, and Ron Guidry, who won 22 games. Then they got one of the best leadoff hitters in the game, who was also the best base-stealer of all time: Rickey Henderson.

Despite the talent, the best the Yankees finished was second place in 1985.

In 1990, the Yankees hit rockbottom, losing 95 games and finishing dead last. They began to rebuild, and by 1993 made another run for the AL Crown.

The Yankees had a good blend of youth and experience. The lineup included Roberto Kelly, Kevin Maas, Don Mattingly, Steve Sax, Danny Tartabull, and Mike Stanley. Pitchers Jimmy Key and Jim Abbott (who threw a no-hitter on September 4) led the team from the mound. But the Toronto Blue Jays pulled ahead and took the division, leaving the Yankees with another second-place finish.

Yankees' first baseman Don Mattingly watches his 200th career home run clear the right-field fence.

Back To The Series

In August 1994, a players' strike ended the baseball season—which meant no postseason play. In 1995, the Yankees finished second in the AL East, but their 79 wins were good enough for a wildcard playoff berth. In the postseason, the Yankees met the Seattle Mariners. New York won the first two games in the five-game series. Seattle fought back to win three-in-a-row and steal the series.

The Yankees added a few players and picked up another American League East Pennant in 1996. Pitchers Andy Pettitte, David Cone, Kenny Rogers, and Dwight Gooden led the solid Yankee staff. Gooden got off to a slow start in 1996, but turned things around on May 14, as he threw his first career no-hitter against the Seattle Mariners, keeping the Yankees on pace to win another AL East title.

Bernie Williams, Tim Raines, Wade Boggs, and Paul O'Neill carried the offensive load. Having won the 1994 batting crown, O'Neill finished in the top five in 1996.

The Yankees also acquired two power-hitting sluggers in Darryl Strawberry and Cecil Fielder around midseason. They were just what the Yankees needed to bring them their 23rd World Series Championship.

In the first round of the 1996 postseason, New York dismantled the Texas Rangers. In the ALCS against Baltimore, the Yanks got some help from an "angel in the outfield." The Orioles were ahead in the eighth inning when Baltimore right fielder Tony Tarasko drifted back to the warning track to catch a flyball off the bat of 1996 AL Rookie of the Year Derek Jeter. Out of nowhere a 12-year-old boy reached over the outfield fence and brought the ball in with his glove. The outfield umpire ruled it a home run and the Yankees went on to win the game and the American League Pennant.

It looked as though the Yankees had fate on their side. Baseball fans across the country were excited to see the Bronx Bombers in the World Series again. Manager Joe Torre had put together a remarkable group of talent that was the sentimental favorite over the defending world champion Atlanta Braves.

But after the first two World Series games in New York, it looked as though the Yankees' luck had run out. In Game 1, Atlanta crushed the Yanks 12-1. Game 2 also saw the Yankees come up short 4-0 at home. The next three games were in Atlanta—and the Braves only needed two victories for the title.

Surprisingly, New York bounced back in Game 3 to win 5-2. But Game 4 looked like an Atlanta blowout. With a 6-0 lead, the Braves were in control. But Yankee determination prevailed. They tied the game 6-6 on a dramatic eighth-inning homer to send the contest into extra innings. And that was all the Yankees needed as they pulled off the biggest come-from-behind victory in World Series history, winning the game 8-6.

In Game 4, Andy Pettitte delivered a gem of a game. He allowed only five hits in eight innings. Pettitte's pitching, supported by great defense and timely hitting, gave the Yankees the close 1-0 win.

The Yanks were now headed back to the Bronx with a 3-2 Series lead—and a lot of confidence. The sixth game went down to the wire, but New York captured the win 3-2, picking up their 23rd World Series Championship.

Another Dynasty?

Could the greatest baseball franchise of all time have the makings of another dynasty? It is hard to say. The Yankees are loaded with great pitching, powerful hitting, spectacular defense, and a great manager.

We know for sure that no team will dominate baseball as the Yankees did from the 1920s through the 1950s. Those kinds of teams we can only read about. But it was fun to see the Yankees do it again in 1996.

Paul O'Neill will try to lead the Yankees to another dynasty.

Glossary

All-Star: A player who is voted by fans as the best player at one position in a given year.

American League (AL): An association of baseball teams formed in 1900 which make up one-half of the major leagues.

American League Championship Series (ALCS): A best-of-seven-game playoff with the winner going to the World Series to face the National League Champions.

Batting Average: A baseball statistic calculated by dividing a batter's hits by the number of times at bat.

Earned Run Average (ERA): A baseball statistic which calculates the average number of runs a pitcher gives up per nine innings of work.

Fielding Average: A baseball statistic which calculates a fielder's success rate based on the number of chances the player has to record an out.

Hall of Fame: A memorial for the greatest baseball players of all time, located in Cooperstown, New York.

Home Run (HR): A play in baseball where a batter hits the ball over the outfield fence scoring everyone on base as well as the batter.

Major Leagues: The highest ranking associations of professional baseball teams in the world, currently consisting of the American and National Baseball Leagues.

Minor Leagues: A system of professional baseball leagues at levels below Major League Baseball.

National League (NL): An association of baseball teams formed in 1876 which make up one-half of the major leagues.

National League Championship Series (NLCS): A best-of-seven-game playoff with the winner going to the World Series to face the American League Champions.

Pennant: A flag which symbolizes the championship of a professional baseball league.

Pitcher: The player on a baseball team who throws the ball for the batter to hit. The pitcher stands on a mound and pitches the ball toward the strike zone area above the plate.

Plate: The place on a baseball field where a player stands to bat. It is used to determine the width of the strike zone. Forming the point of the diamond-shaped field, it is the final goal a base runner must reach to score a run.

RBI: A baseball statistic standing for *runs batted in.* Players receive an RBI for each run that scores on their hits.

Rookie: A first-year player, especially in a professional sport.

Slugging Percentage: A statistic which points out a player's ability to hit for extra bases by taking the number of total bases hit and dividing it by the number of at bats.

Stolen Base: A play in baseball when a base runner advances to the next base while the pitcher is delivering the pitch.

Strikeout: A play in baseball when a batter is called out for failing to put the ball in play after the pitcher has delivered three strikes.

Triple Crown: A rare accomplishment when a single player finishes a season leading their league in batting average, home runs, and RBIs. A pitcher can win a Triple Crown by leading the league in wins, ERA, and strikeouts.

Walk: A play in baseball when a batter receives four pitches out of the strike zone and is allowed to go to first base.

World Series: The championship of Major League Baseball played since 1903 between the pennant winners from the American and National Leagues.

Index

R

Raines, Tim   26
Righetti, Dave   24
Ripken, Cal, Jr.   13
Rivers, Mickey   22
Rogers, Kenny   26
Ruffing, Red   11
Ruth, Babe   7, 8, 10, 17, 20

S

Sax, Steve   25
St. Louis Cardinals   9, 14
Stanley, Mike   25
Steinbrenner, George   22, 24
Stengel, Casey   16, 17
Stottlemyre, Mel   22
Strawberry, Darryl   26

T

Tarasko, Tony   27
Tartabull, Danny   25
Tidrow, Dick   22
Torre, Joe   4, 27

W

White, Roy   22
Williams, Bernie   26
Winfield, Dave   24
World Series   4, 7, 8, 9, 10, 12, 14, 15,
        16, 17, 20, 22, 26, 27
World War II   12

Y

Yankee Stadium   8